date of the day

ayesha erkin

DEDICATION

This series wouldn't exist without my family.

Thank you to my parents and siblings for going along with an idea that they had no clue would take over the Ramadan dinner table for years. For their patience and willingness to try things that brought me joy. Thank you to my cousins and aunts and uncles for joining in without hesitation. For my friends who shared my excitement and have always been available to bounce ideas with me. And especially those who have helped me stay sane in the last few weeks of writing this book.

And a BIG thank you to **you,** for being a part of something I never expected to hilariously lend me the title of "the date girl."

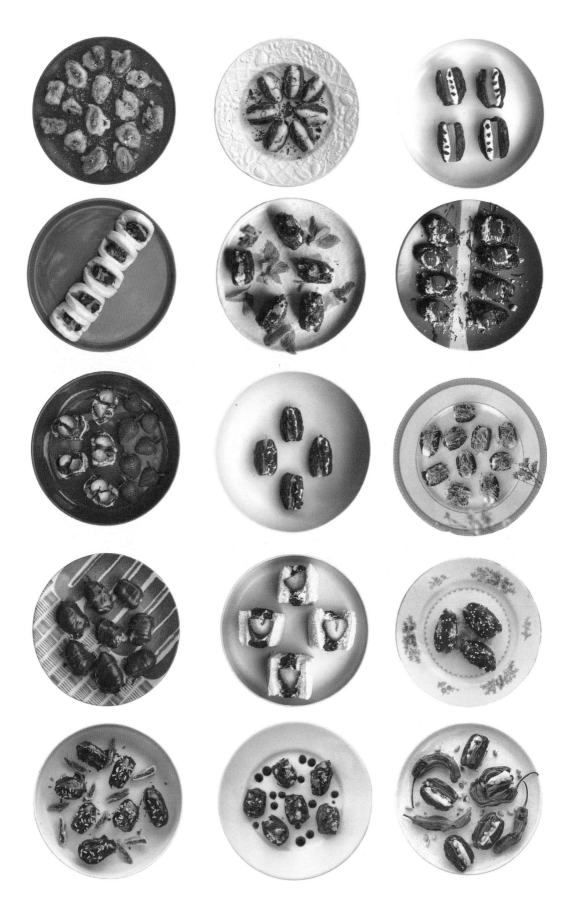

CONTENTS

introduction

"Wait, why are you putting lazajan & chocolate in a date?!" my parents asked skeptically as I urged them to try it. In hindsight, they probably thought I'd finally lost it.

The year 2020 shook us up inside out and upside down. In my case, I decided to pack up my life in Austin, where I'd lived for 5 years, and move in with my parents who had relocated to the greater Dallas area. There was a part of me that felt like I was taking several steps back, having been able to build a life independently outside my family home, achieving the "American Dream". I loved my apartment – Saturday mornings were for cooking brunch while dancing with my cat, Mantu. I'd have friends over for juicy chats as I'd make tea and share treats I stress baked from the weekly trauma working as an architect. I'd spend lazy afternoons laying on my laundry pile straight out of the dryer, alone, watching speckles of sunlight dance through the funky chandelier I hung up in my room. This was *my* home, and I loved it.

But within this life, there were cracks. I spent most of Ramadan feeling depleted, returning home to break my fast alone after working on hot construction sites all day. I would occasionally call my family and eat my meal with them, only to be left with the silence staring at me from the empty chairs at my table. Ramadan is a time for community, and I felt more isolated than ever within the confines of my curated life. So, moving back home before Ramadan during a pandemic was a recipe for something… new?

Ramadan began and I was aimlessly passing time swiping away on Instagram when I saw a post about how the Prophet Mohammad (SAW) used to break his fast with dates and cucumbers. In Islamic tradition, it is customary to break the fast with a date as it is a practice of the Prophet and provides a small yet nutritionally dense bite after a long day of fasting. I was intrigued and immediately prepared a plate of sliced cucumbers with dates to break my fast with. I LOVED it. It was refreshing and crunchy and sweet and gooey and I wanted to eat more things with dates.
This was *fun*.

The next day, I tried dates with other fruits, such as grapes, watermelons, and kiwis. My dad joined in, branching away from his classic but delicious qishta (table cream) and almonds combination. He was surprised by how lovely it tasted. I posted these experiments on social media and immediately received several messages from friends with more suggestions to try.

Ramadan 2020 was the first time in almost a decade that my family of seven was in the same city together. In a way, I had to learn the newer versions of them that I had mostly just met as snippets from visits home. And how else to re-acquaint than by eating with each other? I made a new date combination every day since the original cucumber combo and asked my family to review it alongside me to share online. And that, my friends, is how #DateOfTheDay was born. Four years later, we are forever bonded – maybe a bit traumatized – from tasting over a hundred date combinations.

This book is a compilation of some of the top combinations I've made, but it's also a love letter to my family, friends, and to you – because without you, lovely reader, this series would have been a pandemic experiment and not what it is today. Thank you truly for joining the Erkin family during Ramadan.

Let's have some dates together now, shall we?

how to use
this book

Take this book as a guide.

My diverse culinary background as a serial immigrant mixed TCK (Third Culture Kid) has influenced many of my recipes. Growing up, my family enjoyed a blend of traditional and fusion cuisine, often adapting recipes due to ingredient unavailability. Rather than lamenting over the lack of authentic ingredients, my parents instilled in me the value of adapting and improvising with what is available. This approach has taught me to appreciate ingredients better and embrace culinary experimentation.

My hope is that this book will inspire you to do the same, have fun, and enjoy the culinary journey!

Ingredients

Many of these ingredients can be found readily at the supermarket, but you will need to venture into international stores for some ingredients like sujuk (Turkish sausage) and rose water. I suggest typing something like this when you're doing an online search:

"International Store Near Me"
"Middle Eastern Store Near Me"
"Halal Store Near Me"

I always suggest supporting your local mom n pop shop before going to a big box store, but places like H-Mart and Taj Brothers in the US should have the ingredients you're needing. In the UK, especially in London, I've found most of these ingredients in your local Tesco, Sainsburys or Waitrose – neighborhood depending. I highly suggest first going to your corner shop that's immigrant run as it will likely have the ingredients you're looking for.

Don't be afraid to ask for help when you're looking for something!

dates

A brief history on dates

Dates have been an important food source for humans for thousands of years. They were first cultivated in the Middle East and North Africa over 5,000 years ago and have since spread to many other parts of the world. Dates were highly valued in ancient times, and they were mentioned in many ancient texts and religious scriptures. They were often used as a trade commodity and were even used as currency in some societies. Dates were also an important food for travelers and nomads as they are high in calories, nutrients, and fiber, and they can be stored for a long time without spoiling. Today, dates continue to be a popular food around the world, and they are often used in a variety of dishes, from sweet desserts to savory dishes. Dates are a staple food in the Middle East and have been cultivated there for thousands of years. They are often used in traditional desserts and sweets.

In Islam, dates are mentioned several times in the Quran and are believed to have been one of the favorite foods of the Prophet Mohammad (SAW). Muslims traditionally break their fast with dates during Ramadan.

Types of dates (just a few)

There are a ton of different types of dates and each are unique, but in this book, we're sticking with Medjool as they're the most readily available. I've used Deglet Noor for some of these recipes and they work, but the flavor profile and size is much more mellow than Medjool so you won't taste the date as much. I've standardized most of the recipes to create 10 dates – you can easily half, double, triple or even decuple – we love simple maths.

Have you ever wondered what an **unripe date** looks like?

Medjool: Originally from Morocco, Medjool dates are large, sweet, and chewy with a caramel-like flavor. In the US and UK, They're the easiest to find so we're using them as a default in this book.

Deglet Noor: A popular variety from Tunisia and Algeria, Deglet Noor dates have a light, delicate flavor and a firm, slightly dry texture.

Barhi: Originally from Iraq, Barhi dates are small, round, and golden with a soft, almost creamy texture and a rich, caramel-like flavor.

Zahidi: Originally from Iraq as well, Zahidi dates are small and cylindrical with a smooth, slightly chewy texture and a sweet, nutty flavor. Zahidi translates to something of nobility or scarcity.

Khadrawy: Originally from Iraq and now widely grown in Saudi Arabia, Khadrawy dates are medium-sized, soft, and very sweet with a rich, fruity flavor.

Halawy: A variety grown in several countries, Halawy dates are small to medium-sized with a soft, chewy texture and a sweet, caramel-like flavor.

Sukari: Originating from Saudi Arabia, Sukari dates are medium-sized with a soft, smooth texture and a rich, honey-like flavor with notes of caramel. These are my personal favorite! The name comes from "sukkur", which means sugar in Arabic.

Hayani: Grown in Algeria and Tunisia, Hayani dates are small to medium-sized with a firm, chewy texture and a sweet, nutty flavor.

Mazafati: Originally from Iran, Mazafati dates have a thick flesh and a unique chocolate, brown sugar type flavor.

Thoory: A popular variety in the United States, Thoory dates are small and cylindrical with a firm, chewy texture and a mild, nutty flavor. They origiated from Algeria.

Empress: Known for its large size and sweet, juicy flavor. Originally from Iran, Empress dates are now also grown in California and other parts of the world. They are often used in baking and cooking, as well as enjoyed as a snack on their own.

classic
dates

Welcome to Date Stuffing 101

Before you dive into the main recipes, I recommend starting off with using key ingredients when it comes to stuffing dates. They're a springboard for making your own combinations.
You can't go wrong with these!

Cheeses: Soft cheeses like goat cheese and cream cheese can be used to stuff dates, adding a tangy and creamy flavor to the sweet fruit. Harder cheeses like cheddar or Parmesan can also be used for a more savory option.

Chocolates: Chocolate is a classic filling for dates and can be used in various forms such as melted chocolate chips, chocolate ganache, or even chocolate-hazelnut spread. Chocolate pairs well with nuts, fruits, and cream cheese.

Creams: Creams like mascarpone or clotted cream can add a rich and smooth texture to stuffed dates. They can be mixed with other ingredients like honey or fruit preserves to create a sweet filling.

Fruits: Fresh or dried fruits such as apricots, figs, and cranberries can be chopped up and mixed with nuts or cheese to create a sweet and tangy filling for dates. I love pomegranates and pineapples in dates. I also recommend poaching some fruits with the dates!

Nuts: Nuts such as almonds, walnuts, pecans, pistachios, pine nuts and hazelnuts can be used to add a crunch and nutty flavor to the naturally sweet and soft texture of dates. The nuts can be left whole or chopped.

Nut Butters: Nut butters such as peanut butter, almond butter, and cashew butter can add a creamy texture and rich nutty flavor to stuffed dates. They can be used alone or combined with other ingredients like honey or chocolate to create a delicious filling.

Vegetables: Vegetables like roasted red pepper, jalapeño, and even roasted squash or sweet potato can add a savory element to stuffed dates. These ingredients can be mixed with cheese or nuts for a well-rounded flavor.

Suggestions

You can mix and match with the above ingredients! Some recommendations:

- Peanut Butter + Chocolate
- Almond + Clotted Cream (Baba's OG!)
- Almond Butter, Nutella and Pistachio
- Cream Cheese, Cinnamon + Honey
- Strawberry Jam + Pecans
- PB&J (Peanut Butter + Jelly)
- Poached Pear + Pecans
- Pomegranate + Atayef (ricotta mixed with orange blossom water and sugar syrup)
- (Halal) Bacon wrapped stuffed with cheese
- Creamy Feta + Dill (or other fresh herbs)
- Nut butter, Apple + Roasted Pepita Seeds

sweet
dates

Birthday Cake Crumb Date

It's ironic that I don't care for my birthday, but love birthday cake flavor. This date is inspired by the iconic Christina Tosi's Milk Bar Birthday Cake that I make often. My brother Noman and my best friend Alex both had their birthday during Ramadan, so I made this date specially for them.

10 Medjool dates, pitted

3/4 cup whipped cream, alt: cream cheese, mascarpone, buttercream frosting, clotted cream

Crumble (makes one cup):

1/4 cup granulated sugar

3/4 tbsp light brown sugar

6 tbsp cake flour

1/4 tsp baking powder

1/4 tsp kosher salt

1 tbsp rainbow sprinkles

2 tbsp vegetable oil

1/2 tbsp clear vanilla extract (you can use regular vanilla extract, but it does alter the flavor. Clear vanilla extract gives it that artificial American birthday cake flavor)

Heat the oven to 300F (150 C).

In a medium bowl, combine the sugars, flour, baking powder, salt, and sprinkles, mixing until combined. Add the oil and vanilla and mix again to distribute. The wet ingredients will act as glue to help the dry ingredients form small clusters; continue mixing until this happens.

Spread evenly on an ungreased baking sheet and bake for 15 minutes. Let the rainbow crumbs cool completely.

While the crumbs cool, smear cream into each date. If you'd like a full on birthday cake flavor, you can use buttercream or cream cheese frosting. I personally prefer the lesser sweet creams as the flavor won't empower the crumble.

Serve immediately or refrigerate for up to 3 days. The crumble can be stored for up to 5 days in an airtight container.

Brookie Date

Who doesn't love brownies and cookies?
A faster way to make this is to buy cookie dough and a box brownie mix - stuff the dates with half baked brownies, roll in cookie dough and bake!

10 Medjool dates, pitted

1/2 cup all-purpose flour

1/4 cup unsweetened cocoa powder

1/2 tsp baking powder

1/2 tsp salt

1/2 cup unsalted butter, softened

1/2 cup granulated sugar

1/2 cup light brown sugar

1 egg

1 tsp vanilla extract

1/2 cup chocolate chips

1/2 cup chopped walnuts (optional)

Preheat oven to 350°F (180°C).

In a mixing bowl, whisk together flour, cocoa powder, baking powder, and salt. Set aside.

In another mixing bowl, cream together softened butter, granulated sugar, and light brown sugar until smooth.

Beat in egg and vanilla extract.

Gradually add in flour mixture until well combined. Stir in chocolate chips and chopped walnuts.

Cut dates lengthwise, and flatten slightly.

Stuff each date with a spoonful of brookie dough, then pinch the date closed. Arrange the stuffed dates on a baking sheet lined with parchment paper.

Bake for 15-20 minutes or until golden brown. Let cool for a few minutes before serving. Enjoy!

Cereal Crunch Date

10 medjool dates, pitted and soaked in milk for 30 minutes

1 cup of cereal of your choice (crushed into small pieces) + more for topping

1/2 cup of milk powder

1/4 cup of evaporated milk

Pinch of salt

In a bowl, mix together the crushed cereal, milk powder, evaporated milk, and salt until a thick paste forms. I used Frosted Flakes and Cinnamon Toast Crunch.

Take each milk soaked date and fill it with a small amount of the milk powder paste. You can reuse this milk, it's pretty common to drink date milk!

Pop them in the fridge for about 10 minutes.

Remove and sprinkle cereal on top. Serve!

Note: You can bake these as well at 350°F (180°C) for about 10–12 minutes.

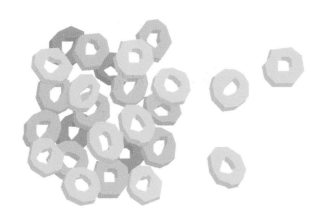

Mango Sticky Rice Date

How can you not love mango sticky rice? This warm glutinous delight pairs well with a date – add some condensed milk on top for a really sticky and sweet treat.

10 Medjool dates, pitted

1 cup glutinous rice

1 can coconut milk

1/4 cup white sugar

1/4 tsp salt

2 ripe mangoes, sliced

Toasted sesame seeds, for garnish

Soak glutinous rice in water for 1 hour.

Drain rice and place in a pot with 1 1/2 cups of water. Bring to a boil, then reduce heat to low and simmer for 20–25 minutes or until rice is cooked and sticky.

In another pot, mix together coconut milk, sugar, and salt. Bring to a boil then remove from heat.

Once the rice is cooked, add half of the coconut milk mixture to the pot and stir until well combined.

Cover the pot and let the rice absorb the coconut milk mixture for 10 minutes.

Fill each date with the sticky rice mixture and a few slices of mango.

Drizzle the remaining coconut milk mixture over the stuffed dates.

Garnish with toasted sesame seeds and serve warm.

Crepe Date

When I studied in Rome for a semester, there was a crepe shop near my flat in Trastevere. They had the richest flavors that sent me into a food coma on our late night sugar craving adventures. But my favorite flavor there was the classic strawberry, banana and nutella crepe.

10 Medjool dates, pitted

2 ripe bananas, sliced

10 fresh strawberries, sliced

1/2 cup all-purpose flour

1/2 cup milk

1 egg

1 tablespoon granulated sugar

1/2 teaspoon vanilla extract

1/4 teaspoon salt

2 tablespoons unsalted butter, melted

Chocolate sauce, for drizzling (you can use nutella)

Powdered sugar, for dusting

Stuff the pitted dates with sliced strawberries and bananas, or any fruit you enjoy with a crepe. You can use chocolate as well.

In a mixing bowl, whisk together the flour, milk, egg, sugar, vanilla extract, salt, and melted butter until smooth.

Preheat a non-stick skillet over medium heat.

Dip the prepared dates in the crepe batter and set aside. Grease the skillet with a little butter or cooking spray.

Using a spoon, pour a small amount of the crepe batter in the pan. It should be about an inch, or the length of your date. Place your dipped date in the center of the poured batter. Cook the crepe for 1–2 minutes, or until the edges start to lift and the bottom is golden brown.

Flip the crepe with the date over and cook for another 1–2 minutes, or until golden brown. You may need to add more batter if the date isn't sticking. Flip all sides until the batter is cooked.

Remove the crepe date from the skillet and repeat with the remaining batter – you can do multiple at the same time but I advise testing one first to adjust temp and amount of batter.

Top your crepe dates with sliced strawberries, powdered sugar and chocolate syrup before serving.

Ferrero Rocher Date

I tested this for Ramadan 2023, and on my 4th year of making date combinations, this one got 10 ACROSS THE BOARD. I was floored. It's THAT good.

10 Medjool dates, pitted

1 cup roughly chopped hazelnuts

1 tbsp cocoa powder

½ teaspoon sea salt

1 cup crushed wafers (I used ice cream wafer cones!)

Chocolate ganache

1 cup chopped bittersweet chocolate or chocolate chips

1 cup heavy cream

To make the **ganache**, add the chocolate and heavy cream in a small saucepan.

Cook on low heat, stirring continuously. You should see it form into a thick chocolate sauce. *Note*: You can adjust the consistency of the ganache by using more or less chocolate or cream. For a thicker ganache, use more chocolate. For a thinner ganache, use more cream.

Remove from heat and pour half of the ganache into a bowl and place in the fridge to cool completely. We want the consistency to be paste-like, as we'll be filling the dates with it. The other half will be for dipping the dates, which should remain a bit more liquid-y. You may need to reheat it on the stovetop or microwave to keep its consistency, but be wary of overheating as the chocolate and cream will separate.

Mix together the crushed wafers, cocoa powder and sea salt.

Assemble the filling station in order of: cold ganache, hazelnuts, warm ganache, crushed wafers cocoa mix.

Spread about a teaspoon of the cold ganache in the date. Sprinkle a teaspoon of hazelnuts inside and squeeze the date shut.

Dip the date in the warm ganache and shake off any excess.

Next, drop the date in the wafer cocoa mix and coat completely. I've found it easier to gently shake the date back and forth in a container with the wafer cocoa mix. Top with hazelnuts, and nutella if you'd like.

Lassi Crème Brûlée Date

The original recipe I made calls for a mango lassi, so add 1 cup ripe (or frozen) mango or ½ cup mango pulp if you'd like to make it that way and reduce the yoghurt to ⅓ cup. You can even make it a Rooh Afza creme brulee!

10 Medjool dates, pitted

3/4 cup greek yoghurt

1-2 tbsp milk or water, as needed

1/2 cup water

2 tsp unflavored gelatin or agar agar (any unflavored thickened agent works)

2-3 threads saffron (or ½ tsp saffron powder)

1 tbsp sugar

1/2 tsp cardamom seeds (or 2-3 cardamom pods)

Dried rose or 1/2 tsp rose water

Cane sugar for sprinkling

Take a small pot and boil water with the saffron, cardamom, dried roses (or rose water) and sugar.

When the water is boiling, add in the gelatin and mix.

Let it cool slightly before placing in the blender with the yoghurt. You want this to be on the thicker side consistency wise as opposed to a regular drinkable lassi, so only add the milk or water as needed but we will be adding the gelatin water mix to this.

Pour into a bowl and place in the fridge for about an hour or two until it's set. You can also place in the freezer for 15-20 minutes if you're in a pinch, but the middle may not set completely.

Take the lassi pudding and place in a piping bag - if you don't have one, place in a ziplock and snip one of the corners for a quick homemade piping bag!

Squeeze the lassi pudding into the dates. The texture should hold easily on its own.
Sprinkle the dates with sugar; I used castor for a richer taste. Using a culinary torch, torch the tops of the dates to create a crispy creme brule type of layer. The sugar is critical for this or you'll just be burning the pudding and date! If you don't have a torch, you can broil it for 30 seconds to 1 minute in the oven or until the top is browned. Be careful to not let it burn.

Place saffron threads or edible rose petals on top to decorate (optional).

S'mores Date

I'm not a huge fan of s'mores, but I am a huge fan of culinary torches and will use one every chance I get. The recipe calls for using the oven as a torch is not a common kitchen tool, but if you have a culinary torch, you can skip putting the dates in the oven and torch them when assembled! I prefer this method as it adds the campfire smokey taste to the dates. Very true to lovable s'mores.

10 medjool dates, pitted

10-20 mini marshmallows or marshmallow puff (you can even use regular ones cut up)

10 small pieces of chocolate (about 1/2 inch squares)

1/4 cup graham cracker crumbs

Sea Salt for sprinkling

Preheat your oven to 350°F (unless using a culinary torch).

Take each pitted date and stuff it with one to two mini marshmallows and one piece of chocolate.

Once all the dates are stuffed, place them on a baking sheet lined with parchment paper.

Sprinkle the graham cracker crumbs over the top of the stuffed dates, pressing them in gently so they stick.

Bake the dates in the preheated oven for 5-7 minutes or until the marshmallows are melted and gooey.

Remove from the oven and let cool for a few minutes before serving. Sprinkle sea salt on top to enhance the chocolate flavor.

Sopapilla Cheesecake Date

If I didn't include this family favorite dessert in a date then I would never hear the end of it. Sopapilla Cheesecake is a dessert my family adopted from a kind neighbor when we moved to the US. You will see it at almost every dinner party. It's actually addicting.

10 medjool dates, pitted

4 oz cream cheese, softened

1/4 cup granulated sugar

1 teaspoon vanilla extract

1 can crescent roll dough

2 tablespoons unsalted butter, melted

1/4 cup cinnamon sugar

Preheat your oven to 350°F (180°C)

In a medium bowl, beat the cream cheese, granulated sugar, and vanilla extract until smooth.

Using a small spoon, stuff each pitted date with the cream cheese mixture.

Unroll the crescent roll dough and divide it into 10 equal triangles.

Roll each stuffed date in one triangle of dough, making sure to cover it completely. Place the wrapped dates on a baking sheet lined with parchment paper.

Brush the melted butter over the top of each wrapped date.

Sprinkle the cinnamon sugar evenly over the top of each wrapped date.

Bake for 12–15 minutes, or until the crescent roll dough is golden brown and the cream cheese filling is warm and gooey.

Remove from the oven and let cool for a few minutes before serving.

Sticky Toffee Pudding Date

A very British dessert that I was unaware of until summer '21 and have been hooked on ever since. When I learned this dessert is made with dates, I spent some time in the kitchen dissecting each ingredient to see how to create the gooey texture sans dates.... so I could stuff it in a date.

10 Medjool dates, pitted

1/2 cup all-purpose flour

1/2 tsp baking powder

1/4 tsp baking soda

1/4 tsp salt

1/4 cup unsalted butter, softened

1/2 cup brown sugar

1 large egg

1 tsp vanilla extract

1/2 cup boiling water

1/2 cup heavy cream

1/2 cup brown sugar

1/4 cup unsalted butter

1/4 tsp salt

Vanilla ice cream, for serving (optional, but recommended)

Preheat oven to 350°F (180°C). Grease a baking dish that can fit all the dates.

In a medium bowl, whisk together flour, baking powder, baking soda, and salt.
In a large bowl, cream together the butter and brown sugar until light and fluffy. Beat in the egg and vanilla.

Gradually mix in the dry ingredients until just combined. Stir in boiling water.
Divide the batter among the pitted dates, filling each date about 2/3 full.

Bake for 20–25 minutes or until the pudding is set and the tops are golden brown.

While the dates are baking, prepare the toffee sauce. In a small saucepan, combine cream, brown sugar, butter, and salt. Heat over medium heat, stirring occasionally, until the butter is melted and the sugar is dissolved.

Reduce the heat to low and simmer for 5–7 minutes or until the sauce has thickened. Drizzle toffee sauce on top of the dates, making sure the cake part absorbs it by letting them sit for a few minutes.

Serve the baked dates with warm toffee sauce and vanilla ice cream.

savory
dates

Avocado Toast Date

If you love avocado and Everything But The Bagel, this date is for you! The garlic does have a storng flavor, so omit it if you'd rather it be subtle.

10 Medjool dates, pitted

1 ripe avocado

1 small garlic clove, minced (optional)

1 tablespoon fresh lime juice

Salt and pepper to taste

Toasted sesame seeds or everything bagel seasoning, for topping

Preheat the oven to 350°F (180°C).

Cut the avocado in half and remove the pit. Scoop out the flesh and mash it in a bowl.

Add the minced garlic, lime juice, salt, and pepper to the mashed avocado and mix well.

Stuff each date with the avocado mixture using a spoon.

Sprinkle the stuffed dates with sesame seeds or everything bagel seasoning.

Place the stuffed dates on a baking sheet lined with parchment paper.

Bake in the preheated oven for 5–7 minutes or until the dates are slightly softened and the topping is golden brown. Serve warm.

Za'atar & Feta F'teer Date

Please go buy za'atar at a Middle Eastern store! You won't regret it. The ones at places like Trader Joes are so bland. Plus, you'd be supporting local! Best to get fresh za'atar if you can.

10 medjool dates, pitted

2 tablespoons za'atar*

2 tablespoons crumbled feta cheese

1 tablespoon olive oil

F'teer dough (store bought or homemade; you can also use phyllo. Not the same, but close)

Vegetable oil for frying

Preheat the oven to 350°F (180 C).

In a small bowl, mix together the zaatar spice blend and crumbled feta cheese. Stuff each date with a small amount of the zaatar-feta mixture.

Roll out the f'teer dough into a thin sheet, and cut into circles or squares that are slightly larger than the stuffed dates.

Wrap each stuffed date in a piece of f'teer dough, folding the dough around the date and pinching the edges to seal.

Heat vegetable oil in a large pan over medium-high heat.

Fry the stuffed dates in batches until golden brown and crispy, about 2-3 minutes per side. Drain the fried dates on paper towels to remove excess oil.

Drizzle olive oil over the fried dates and sprinkle with any remaining zaatar-feta mixture.

Bake the stuffed and fried dates in the preheated oven for 5-7 minutes to crisp up the f'teer dough.

Serve warm and enjoy!

Bao Date

You ever just walk around a grocery store and all of a sudden inspiration strikes? The bao date came about from my monthly H Mart stroll. Sipping on my bubble tea, I saw frozen bao buns and immediately thought "Can I put this in a date?!"

10 Medjool dates, pitted

10 thin slices of beef steak

1 medium carrot, sliced into thin strips

1/2 medium cucumber, sliced into thin strips

10 small bao buns

Fresh cilantro leaves for garnish

Marinade for beef:

1 tablespoon soy sauce

1 tablespoon oyster sauce

1 teaspoon sugar

1/2 teaspoon sesame oil

In a small bowl, whisk together the marinade ingredients.

Preheat a grill pan or skillet over medium-high heat.

Place the beef slices in a shallow dish and pour the marinade over them. Let marinate for 10–15 minutes.

Wrap each date with a slice of beef steak, securing it with a toothpick.

Grill the wrapped dates for 2–3 minutes on each side, or until the beef is cooked to your desired doneness.

Steam the bao buns according to package instructions.

Fill each steamed bao bun with a wrapped date, carrot and cucumber slices, and top with cilantro leaves. Serve warm.

Cacık Date

Featured on Bon Appetit! This recipe makes enough cacik to stuff 20+ Medjool dates, so reduce if you'd like less cacik. This Cacik is also thicker and garlic-less, which is a key ingredient traditionally, however, it overpowers the date in this instance so I recommend omitting or adding it to the leftover cacik.

20 medjool dates (or less, you'll just have leftover cacik which is also great)

1 small cucumber

Half a lemon

1/2 tsp salt

1/2 tsp black pepper

1/2 tsp sumac

1 tbsp dried mint

1 cup greek yogurt

Handful of fresh mint for garnishing

Fresh dill (optional – I prefer the mint with the date)

1 tbsp olive oil (can omit if using chili oil)

Crispy chili oil (optional – I used homemade, but easily found in store!)

SCAN FOR RECIPE VIDEO

Pit your medjool dates and set aside.

Dice the cucumber and place in a bowl. Squeeze the lemon and add the seasoning to the same bowl. Let it sit for a few minutes for the cucumber to absorb the spices and then add in the yogurt.

Cacik is typically thinner, but for it to hold well in the date, we opted for greek yogurt and will not add any additional water or ice.
Mix well, toss in the fresh mint. You can use fresh dill as well, which is often used in cacik, but can overpower the date.

Take your pitted dates and spoon in the cacik. Place aside or in the fridge.

Drizzle with olive oil if you omit the chili oil topping. I don't recommend doing both as each oil has their own distinct tastes, so it would clash.

Heat up your chili oil crisp in a pan for 30 seconds or until you hear a sizzle. Immediately remove from heat as you do not want to add a burnt taste. I recommend using a chili crisp with less garlicky flavor.

Drizzle the chili crisp and oil over the dates, top with fresh herbs (mint or dill or both!) and serve immediately.

Chicken & Waffles Date

So I may have had an obsession with the air fryer and therefore there was a period of air frying everything, including dates. 10/10 machine, highly recommend.

10 Medjool dates, pitted

1 chicken breast, cut into small pieces

1/2 cup all-purpose flour

1/2 cup buttermilk

1/2 cup panko breadcrumbs

1 tsp paprika

1/2 tsp salt

1/4 tsp black pepper

Cooking spray

3 frozen waffles, toasted

Maple syrup, for serving

Preheat the air fryer to 400°F (200°C).

In three separate shallow bowls, place flour, buttermilk, and breadcrumbs.

Add paprika, salt, and black pepper to the breadcrumbs bowl and mix well.

Dip each chicken piece into the flour, then buttermilk, and finally into the seasoned breadcrumbs.

Place the chicken pieces into the air fryer basket, lightly coat them with cooking spray, and cook for 8–10 minutes or until the chicken is crispy and cooked through.

While the chicken is cooking, slice each date in half and remove the pit. Place one piece of chicken onto each date half.

Toast the waffles and cut each one into small squares.

Place one waffle square on top of each chicken piece.

Drizzle each date with maple syrup and serve immediately. Enjoy!

Corn Dog Dates

One of my favorite after school snacks in high school were the vegan Morning Glory corn dogs. I'd pop one in the oven and slather it in ketchup while watching Potter Puppet Pals on repeat. Good ole days.

10 medjool dates, pitted

10 mini hot dogs (or 3 normal ones sliced in quarters), pre-cooked. They can even be vegan ones.

1/2 cup cornmeal

1/2 cup all-purpose flour

1 tsp baking powder

1/4 tsp salt

1/4 tsp black pepper

1/4 cup milk

1 egg, beaten

1 tbsp honey

Vegetable oil, for frying
Cake Pop or Wooden Skewers

Cut the skewers to be about 3 inches (8 cm) long.

Cut a small slit in each date and stuff with a mini hot dog, sliced to the size of the date so it fits snugly. Skewer the date in the middle, piercing the hot god and making sure it's secure.

In a bowl, whisk together the cornmeal, flour, baking powder, salt, and black pepper.

In another bowl, whisk together the milk, egg, and honey.

Add the wet ingredients to the dry ingredients and stir until combined.
Heat about 2-3 inches (5 - 8 cm) of vegetable oil in a large pot over medium-high heat.

Dip each stuffed date into the cornmeal batter and gently shake off any excess.
Fry the dates in the hot oil, turning occasionally, until golden brown and crispy, about 2-3 minutes.

Use a slotted spoon to transfer the corn dog dates to a paper towel-lined plate to drain any excess oil.

Let them cool and serve with maple syrup if you want something a bit sweeter, or mustard and ketchup if you want to go all in!

Crispy Cheese & Dill Dates

10 Medjool dates, pitted

1 cup grated cheddar cheese

1/4 cup chopped fresh dill

1/4 tsp garlic powder

Salt and pepper to taste

Ranch, for serving (optional)

Preheat your oven to 350°F (175°C).

In a mixing bowl, combine the grated cheddar cheese, chopped fresh dill, garlic powder, salt, and pepper.

Mix well to combine.

Stuff the mixture into each of the pitted dates, packing it in tightly.

Place the stuffed dates on a baking sheet lined with parchment paper.

Bake in the preheated oven for 10–15 minutes or until the cheese is melted and crispy.

Remove from the oven and let cool for a few minutes. Serve warm. Pairs well with ranch!

Halloumi & Honey Chili Oil Dates

I love chili oil. I put it on everything. My Uyghur grandmother is the reason for this. Lazajan is an Uyghur chili oil that is a staple in the Erkin household. We make it in bulk because panic will ensue if we don't have any. The fridge is never without butter, evaporated milk and lazajan.

10 Medjool dates, pitted

100g halloumi cheese, cut into small cubes

2 tablespoons of chili oil

2 tablespoons of honey

Preheat the oven to 180°C (350°F).

Stuff each date with a small cube of halloumi cheese.

Drizzle 1/2 teaspoon of chili oil over each date.

Place the stuffed dates onto a baking tray lined with parchment paper.

Bake for 5–7 minutes, or until the cheese is melted and the dates are slightly caramelized.

Drizzle 1/2 teaspoon of honey over each date. Best served warm.

Labne, Sweet Potato, Pomegranate & Fried Sage Date

Inspired by fall flavors, this is a pretty sophisticated combination that will impress your guests. The ingredients together look beautiful since the colors contrast well. Looks good and tastes good – a winner.

10 Medjool dates, pitted

1/2 cup labne

1/2 roasted sweet potatoes, cut into the size of the date

1/4 cup pomegranate seeds

10 sage leaves

1/2 cup butter

Sea salt for sprinkling

Smear labne on the inside half of the date.

Place the roasted sweet potato in the other half. Top with pomegranate seeds.

In a small saucepan, brown the butter over medium–high heat.

Once the oil is hot, fry the sage leaves until crispy, about 1–2 minutes per side.

Use a slotted spoon to remove the sage leaves from the oil and place them on a paper towel to drain any excess oil.

Garnish each stuffed date with a fried sage leaf.

Serve immediately or store in the refrigerator for up to 2 days.

Tahini, Sea Salt & Mint Date

If you're not a tahini lover, I recommend mixing it with some honey. However, these three ingredients play up really nicely with the date, especially served chilled.

10 medjool dates, pitted

1/4 cup tahini

1/4 teaspoon sea salt

10 small fresh mint leaves

In a small bowl, mix together the tahini and sea salt until well combined.

Stuff each date with about 1/2 teaspoon of the tahini mixture, using a small spoon or your fingers to gently press it into the center of the date.

Place the stuffed dates on a baking sheet lined with parchment paper.

Garnish each date with a small mint leaf on top of the tahini mixture.

Serve immediately or store in an airtight container in the refrigerator for up to 5 days.

Enjoy these delicious and healthy stuffed medjool dates with tahini, sea salt, and fresh mint!

combo dates

Brown Butter Pretzel Crunch Date

I love brown butter so much. it's a simple way to add depth to sweet or savory dishes. It's easier to make than it seems – just keep an eye on the heat and use your sense of smell so it doesn't burn!

10 Medjool dates, pitted

1/2 cup crushed pretzels

1/4 cup unsalted butter

1/4 cup brown sugar

1/4 cup heavy cream

1/2 tsp sea salt

In a small saucepan, melt the butter over medium heat. Once melted, continue to stir frequently until the butter turns golden brown and smells nutty, about 5-7 minutes.

Add brown sugar, heavy cream, and sea salt to the browned butter. Cook over medium heat, stirring constantly, until the sugar has dissolved and the mixture has thickened, about 5 minutes. Remove from heat and let cool for a few minutes.

Take a pitted date and stuff it with a small amount of the pretzel crunch. Then, generously drizzle the date with the brown butter salted caramel sauce. Top with more crushed pretzels.

Serve warm or cold.

Camembert Cocoa Pastry Date

My mom loved this one from 2021, so I had to include it for her :)

10 medjool dates

1 round of Camembert cheese

1 sheet of puff pastry, thawed

1/4 cup honey

1 tablespoon cocoa powder, preferably Dutch processed

½ cup melted butter

Preheat the oven to 375°F (190°C).

Cut the puff pastry into 10 squares.

Cut the Camembert cheese into small cubes.

Pit the dates and stuff each one with a cube of Camembert cheese.

Place each stuffed date on top of a puff pastry square and fold the corners of the pastry up around the date.

Brush each pastry with butter.

Bake for 20-25 minutes or until the pastry is golden brown.

While the pastries are baking, mix together the honey and cocoa powder in a small bowl.

Once the pastries are done, drizzle them with the honey-cocoa mixture.
Serve warm and enjoy!

Coconut Pakora Date

This is an actual dish from the Malabar region in Kerala, India. It's known as Khajur Bhajiya and it's a Ramadan specialty that's enjoyed with a cup of chai. I stuffed some coconut butter, almonds and cashews on the inside and, of course, had it with a chai.

10 Medjool dates, pitted

1 cup shredded coconut

1 cup white flour

2–3 tbsp wheat or chickpea flour

1/4 teaspoon baking soda

1/2 teaspoon salt

1/2 teaspoon cardamom powder

1/2 cup water

1/2 cup coconut butter

1/2 cup cashews

1/2 cup almonds

Oil for frying

In a mixing bowl, combine the shredded coconut, flour, wheat flour, baking powder, salt, and cardamom powder.

Add water gradually and mix until it forms a thick batter. Set aside.

Stuff coconut butter and nuts into the dates.

Take one date at a time and dip it into the batter, making sure it is fully coated.

Heat oil in a pan or a deep fryer.

Gently drop the dates into the hot oil and fry them until they are golden brown.

Use a slotted spoon to remove the dates from the oil and place them on a paper towel to remove excess oil.

Serve hot with chutney or dipping sauce of your choice.

Everything But The Kitchen Sink Date

This date is based off of one of my favorite cookies, Everything But The Kitchen Sink, which sounds exactly as it is. It's a mashup of sweet and salty textural fun that translates really well stuffed in a date!

10 Medjool dates, pitted

1/2 cup creamy peanut butter

1/2 cup crushed pretzels

1/2 cup crushed potato chips

1/4 cup mini M&M's

1/4 cup edible coffee beans

In a small bowl, mix together the peanut butter, crushed pretzels, crushed potato chips, M&M's, and edible coffee beans until well combined.

Take a pitted date and stuff it with the peanut butter mixture, using a small spoon or your fingers to press the mixture into the date.

Repeat with the remaining dates.

Serve and enjoy! These can be stored in an airtight container in the refrigerator for up to a week.

Kashmiri Chai Panna Cotta Date

This is one of those recipes that is a base for you to try with others – I've made this exact one with different types of tea and coffee. But I love the Kashmiri Chai version because the tea is traditionally made with salt and I enjoy the contrast with the date.

10 medjool dates, pitted

Crushed pistachios, for sprinkling

Sea salt, for sprinkling

Chai Panna Cotta:

1 cup heavy cream

1/2 cup milk

1/2 cup Kashmiri chai concentrate without milk

1 –2 tbsp sugar

2 tsp gelatin (or 1 tsp agar agar)

Notes on Kashmiri Chai:
- The traditional way to make Kashmiri chai, or noon chai, is with salt.
- You can find a recipe for the concentrate on my website that my great aunt taught me how to make as she married into a Kashmiri family. Just don't add the milk.
- You can buy a powdered version of Kashmiri chai, but it's generally a sweetened one. In a pinch, it works but make sure to add salt!

Add cream, milk, chai concentrate and gelatin to a pot on medium heat. Mix and keep stirring until it comes to a boil. Remove from heat and set aside for 10 minutes.

Add sugar and mix well until the panna cotta is almost boiling. This is where you need to taste to adjust. The color should be a dusty pink.

Pour into a container and once at room temp, place the panna cotta in the fridge for 3–4 hours until set.

Once set, scoop out about a spoonful and stuff the panna cotta in the dates. The panna cotta should be firm, but have a creamy feel. It should sit in the date without spilling over. If it's too liquid like, allow it to set for longer or reheat and add more gelatin or agar agar.

Top with crushed pistachios and sea salt and serve.

Mint Labneh & Rose Jam Date

Labneh is a type of yoghurt cheese that's commonly eaten in the Middle East. The flavor is tangy and the texture is creamy. It goes really well with sweet and savory foods. Rose Jam is a Turkish jam and can be found easily in International stores.

10 Medjool dates, pitted

1/2 cup labneh

1/4 cup chopped fresh mint leaves

2 tablespoons rose jam

1/4 teaspoon ground cinnamon

In a small mixing bowl, combine the labneh, chopped mint leaves, and cinnamon.

Stuff each date with about a teaspoon of the labneh mixture.

Drizzle the rose jam mixture over the stuffed dates.

Top with fresh mint. Serve cold for a refreshing bite.

Miso Caramel Date

Salty, sweet, rich rich umami flavor in this one. it's surprisingly versatile as well – feel free to stuff something in the date!

10 Medjool dates, pitted

1/2 cup granulated sugar

1/4 cup water

1/4 cup heavy cream

1 tablespoon white miso paste

Pinch of sea salt flakes

Optional Stuffing:

- **I stuffed the date with heavy cream and froze it for 5 minutes before dipping in the caramel. It's a nice surprise.**
- **Cheesecake would be delicuous in this**
- **Mochi**
- **Wafer cookies**
- **Red bean paste (acquired taste, but it's great)**

In a medium saucepan, combine the sugar and water over medium heat. Cook, stirring occasionally, until the sugar has dissolved.

Increase the heat to high and bring the mixture to a boil. Do not stir the mixture anymore at this point.

Cook until the mixture turns a deep amber color, about 7–10 minutes.

Remove the saucepan from heat and carefully whisk in the heavy cream.

Whisk in the miso paste until well combined.

Stir in a pinch of sea salt flakes.

Allow the caramel to cool for a few minutes, then dip the dates in the caramel. Sprinkle more sea salt flakes on top if you'd like.

Place on a parchment paper and refrigerate to firm up.

Serve immediately or chill in the fridge for up to 2 days.

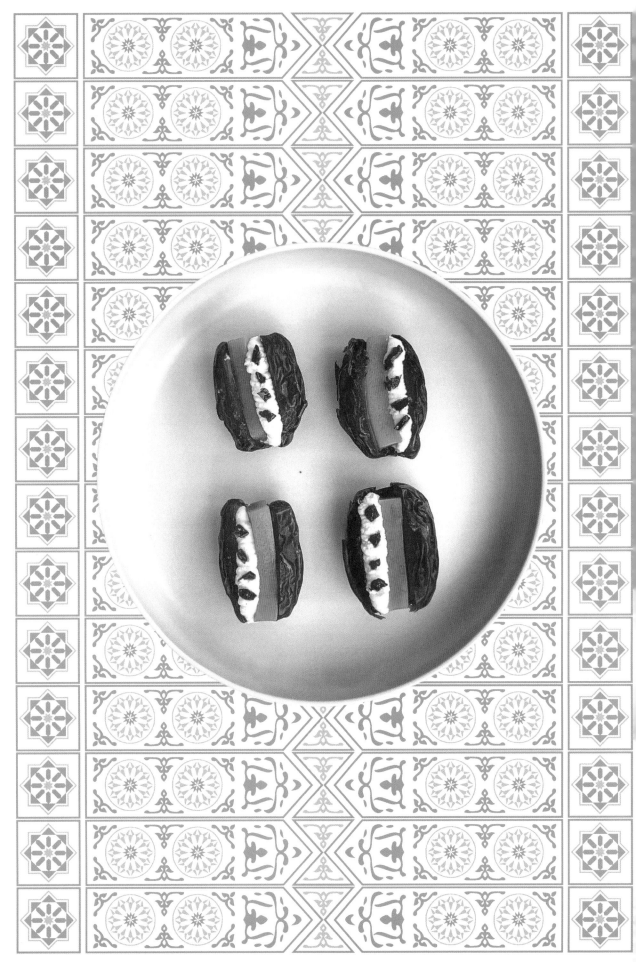

Pandan Jelly, Coconut Cream & Burnt Sugar Date

I am no expert when it comes to South East Asian flavors, but I adore Pandan. The grassy vanilla like flavor adds so much to any dish. This recipe is a bit laborious but my parents, who have never had pandan before, loved it.

10 medjool dates, pitted
1/4 cup condensed milk (optional)

Pandan Jelly:
1 cup pandan juice
1/2 cup sugar
1/2 teaspoon salt
2 1/2 teaspoons agar agar powder
1/2 cup water

Whipped Coconut Cream:
1 can (13.5 oz) coconut milk, chilled in frdige overnight

Burnt Sugar:
1/2 cup brown sugar
1/4 cup hot water

Notes on Pandan:
- For this recipe, I used canned pandan juice from the Asian market as I couldn't find the leaves. Make sure the only ingredients are pandan leaves and water. But always use the leaves when you can!

Notes on coconut milk:
- Use fall fat coconut milk.
- You MUST refrigerate overnight or the creamy part won't seperate as well.
- If your coconut whipped cream is too stiff when whipping, add some of the reserved liquid from the can to help it blend smoother and create more air.
- Can be made in advance and stored in the fridge, which will firm it up.

Make the **pandan jelly** by combining pandan juice, sugar, and salt in a saucepan. Stir well and bring to a boil over medium heat.

In a separate bowl, whisk together agar agar powder and water until well combined. Add the agar agar mixture to the pandan juice mixture and stir well to combine.

Cook the mixture over medium heat, stirring constantly, until the agar agar is fully dissolved and the mixture thickens slightly, about 5 minutes.

Remove the mixture from the heat and pour it into a container. Allow it to cool to room temperature before transferring it to the fridge to set for at least 2 hours or until fully set. When set, slice the pandan jelly into slivers the size of the date and set aside.

Make the **burnt sugar** by combining 1/2 cup brown sugar and 1/4 cup hot water in a small saucepan. Cook over medium heat, stirring constantly, until the sugar has dissolved and the mixture starts to thicken and turn amber in color. Remove the pan from the heat and let it cool slightly. When hardened, break the sugar into small pieces.

Make the **coconut cream** by scooping out the solid part of the coconut milk can and using an electric whisk, whip until there are soft peaks.

Stuff each date with a sliver of pandan jelly and pipe in another line of the whipped coconut cream. Place the burnt sugar over the stuffed dates and serve immediately. If you'd like a bit more sweetness, drizzle condensed milk on top.

Pineapple Tajin Date

Tajin is a staple in Texas. It is a popular Mexican spice blend made with a combination of salt, chili peppers, and dehydrated lime. Warming up the date with this crunchy, juicy and spicy mix is a delight. But you can just stuff a date with pineapple and sprinkle tajin on top and it's equally worth trying.

10 Medjool dates, pitted

1/2 cup diced fresh pineapple

1 tsp Tajin seasoning (recipe below, or just use chili powder, salt and lime)

1 tbsp honey

1/4 cup chopped roasted almonds

Homemade Tajin:

1 tbsp cayenne powder

1 tbsp guajillo powder

2 tbsp crystalized lime powder

2 tbsp salt

1 tbsp sugar

Homemade Tajin: Mix the spices together and store in an airtight container.

Preheat oven to 350°F (180°C).

Stuff each date with a piece of diced pineapple.

Sprinkle the Tajin seasoning over the stuffed dates.

Drizzle the honey over the dates and sprinkle the chopped almonds on top.

Place the stuffed dates on a baking sheet and bake for 10-12 minutes or until the dates are warmed through and the almonds are lightly toasted.

Serve warm as a sweet and spicy snack or dessert. Enjoy!

Peppers & Honey Date

Shishito peppers are a fun food to eat together. It's the luck of the draw – who gets the spicy one?! Spice it up even more and put this combination in your dates and wait until someone get's a scorcher.

10 medjool dates, pitted

1 cup shishito peppers

4 oz Brie cheese, cut into small pieces

2 tbsp honey

2 tbsp pine nuts

1 tbsp olive oil

Salt and pepper to taste

Heat the olive oil in a skillet over medium-high heat. Add the shishito peppers and cook, stirring occasionally, until blistered and softened, about 5–7 minutes.

Remove the peppers from the heat and let them cool.

Toast the pine nuts in the same pan and set aside.

In a small bowl, mix the Brie cheese and honey together until well combined.

Take a pitted date and stuff it with a piece of the cheese mixture and a few shishito peppers. Repeat with the remaining dates. Sprinkle the stuffed dates with toasted pine nuts and season with salt and pepper to taste.

Serve immediately or refrigerate until ready to serve.

bonus dates

Donut.
Lotus Coffee Crunch.
Jammy Onions.

+ five more well loved dates.

I call these 8 the bonus track – from the last 3 years, they're the dates that warranted a "RECIPE PLEASE", so I filmed them.

and now wrote them.

So, you have both!

Donut Date

I first made this in 2020, and it is still a crowd favorite. It's one of my favorite dates to make for a large crowd since it's easy and, well, tastes like donuts! My sister Mariam suggested it, so credit goes to her cause she loves donuts.

10 Medjool dates, pitted

A sweet, soft bread. I recommend using milk bread or brioche or Hawaiian rolls. Even croissants would work.

1/2 cup (64 g) powdered sugar, plus more to thicken glaze as needed

1 tbsp milk (15 ml), plus more to thin glaze as needed

1/2 tsp (2 ml) vanilla extract

1/2 tsp (2ml) lemon juice

Sprinkles to decorate (highly recommended)

Place powdered sugar, milk, vanilla and lemon into a bowl and whisk until it's at a medium consistency with a shiny glaze. To adjust if too thick or too runny, add more milk or sugar accordingly.

Take your bread and rip a piece of. Compress it with your hands until it feels pretty dense. Stuff it into the date, adding more as needed but don't overstuff as you want to make sure the opening of the date can close! This is because if you dip it into the glaze and too much gets into the bread, it'll be too sweet and the texture will be off.

Place the dipped dates on some parchment paper and decorate with sprinkles immediately before the glaze dries.

Let the glaze dry at room temp (approx. 1 hour) or place in the fridge to speed up the process.

Enjoy with some coffee!

SCAN FOR RECIPE VIDEO

Earl Grey & Lavender Fudge Date

10 Medjool dates, pitted

4 to 5 Dried Figs

Dried lavender, for sprinkling

Fudge Sauce:

2 tbsp Steeped Earl grey tea (two teabags)

1 tbsp Lavender syrup

30 g Dark chocolate (I used 72%, you can use whatever chocolate you like!)

18 g Dutch processed cocoa powder

2 tbsp Agave Syrup/ Corn Syrup/ Maple Syrup (glucose, basically)

20 g sugar

55 g heavy cream

1 g Sea salt

Flour to thicken, as needed

Boil some water and pour in a mug with two Earl Grey tea bags. let tea steep for 5–7 minutes until color is dark golden and the aroma is strong.

Add tea in a bowl with the cocoa powder, chopped chocolate and salt.

In a heavy bottomed saucepan, add the cream, syrup, sugar and lavender syrup. Bring to a boil on high heat.

Once boiled, immediately pour it into the bowl with the chocolate and let sit for one minute.

Begin whisking the mixture until silky smooth and glossy. This can take 3–6 minutes, depending on how fast you whisk.

If the mixture is too runny, add some flour 1 tbsp. at a time. If too thick, add a bit of hot water or cream.

Add the sliced figs inside the date. Dip in the fudge sauce. Top with dried lavender. Pop it in the fridge for 1–2 hours and serve!

SCAN FOR RECIPE VIDEO

Jammy Onions & Mascarpone Date

Listen – I know, onions and dates?! It's not as wild as you think. This is one of my favorite recipes and surprises everyone! if you want more of a kick, use a stronger cheese, like blue cheese or kashkaval, in place of the mascarpone.

7 to 10 Medjool dates

Mascarpone spread (or any type of cream spread that's not too sweet)

1/2 white or yellow onion

1 tbsp ghee

1 tbsp honey (I used a light and a dark honey for contrast!)

Water (as needed)

Chop onions thinly

Heat pan to medium heat and add ghee. Immediately add half a tablespoon of honey to the ghee. I used a light flowery one for this.

Add the onions and lower heat. You're not sautéing the onions! You want them to cook slowly for them to caramelize.

If it looks like they're getting crisp, pour some water on the onions. This helps soften them!

When slightly brown and soft, add the other half of the honey. When a jammy texture is achieved, remove from heat. Taste (if you can) and adjust sweetness accordingly.

Set aside to cool. While the onions are cooling, slice and pit the dates. Once pitted, add a smear of mascarpone to one half of the interior of the date.

Scoop some onions and fill in the other half. Serve immediately and enjoy! This can be stored in the fridge for about 3-4 days.

SCAN FOR RECIPE VIDEO

Knafeh Date

10 Medjool dates, pitted

Attar (sugar syrup):
1/2 cup water (4 oz)
1/2 cup sugar (100 g)
1 tbsp fresh lemon (14 g)
1 tbsp rose water (14 g)
1 tbsp orange blossom water (14 g)
Rose petals (optional)

Kaitafi (shredded phyllo dough):
20 g Kataifi, defrosted
1 tbsp (14 g) ghee (butter ghee)
1/2 tsp (4 g) red or orange food color
Crushed pistachios (optional)

Filling:
Sweet Cheese (this is found in Arab stores and literally called Sweet Cheese. But you can use Akawi, nabulsi or mozzarella. Or mix them!)

Place all the attar ingredients in a pot and mix until the sugar is dissolved and it comes to a boil.

When slightly cooled, place the dates in the pot and let it soak for about 30 minutes.

Slice the cheese to fit in the dates. Be a little generous.

Chop up the Kataifi. Try to keep the stars to about an inch.

Melt ghee and let the food coloring bloom in the melted ghee and mix. Pour over the Kataifi and mix with your hands until blended.

Strain the dates. Keep the attar, you'll need it for the last step! Remove the pits and peel the skin off if it's flaky.

Place cheese in dates and then top with the Kataifi.

Place in a preheated oven at 200 C/ 365 F for about 10–15 minutes.

Remove from oven and immediately drizzle sheets syrup on top while it's hot.

SCAN FOR RECIPE VIDEO

Lotus Coffee Crunch Date

I don't know how Muslims became obsessed with Lotus (Biscoff) spread, but it's somehow become as iconic as Rooh Afza and Vimto. Understandbly, it is delicious.

7 to 10 medjool dates

A strong shot of coffee. (I used 2 tsp instant coffee in an espresso cup)

2 oz (approx 50-60 g) boiled water for the instant coffee

1/2 cup mascarpone or any type of mildly sweet cream

Lotus spread

Crunchy granola (around 1/4 cup / 32 g)

Boil water and make your coffee. You can make any type you like! I used instant as it's quick but other options can be slow drip, Turkish or Arabic coffee.

While the coffee cools to room temp, remove the pits from the dates.

Stuff the dates with lotus spread.
Scoop the mascarpone into a bowl and pour in the cooled coffee.

Whip until there are no clumps and the color is golden. Feel free to add any extra flavoring like cardamom powder or syrups if you'd like!

Dip your dates in the coffee cream. Place on wax or parchment paper and sprinkle with the granola.

Melt about a tablespoon of lotus spread in the microwave. Use it to decorate the top of the dates

Place dates in the fridge for at least one hour to set. These should stay good for a few days but make sure to store them in the refrigerator. Enjoy!

SCAN FOR RECIPE VIDEO

Millionaire Shortbread Date

If I could rename this one, I'd call it a Twix date. It's one of my personal favorites and is so over the top indulgent that I recommend waiting to have this when you know you're prepared for a sugar crash.

10 Medjool dates, pitted
Sea salt, for sprinkling

Shortbread (or you can buy premade)
1 cup unsalted butter, softened
1 tbsp granulated sugar
1 tbsp light brown sugar, packed
1 large egg yolk
1 teaspoon vanilla extract
1/2 teaspoon salt
1 11/4 cups all-purpose flour

Chocolate
2 cups semisweet chocolate chips
1/2 cup heavy cream
1/2 teaspoon vanilla extract

Caramel (or you can purchase non high fructose ones as they won't set)
One 14-oz cans sweetened condensed milk
1 cup butter
1/2 cup light brown sugar packed
1/4 cup light corn syrup
1 teaspoon vanilla extract
1/2 teaspoon salt

Preheat the oven to 350°F (180 C)

Make the **shortbread**: In a large bowl, cream together the butter, granulated sugar, and light brown sugar until light and fluffy. Beat in the egg yolk and vanilla extract. Add the salt and flour, and mix until just combined.

Spread the shortbread dough evenly onto a parchment-lined 8x8-inch baking dish. Bake for 20–25 minutes, or until golden brown. Allow to cool completely.

Make the **caramel**: In a medium saucepan, melt the butter over medium heat. Stir in the brown sugar, corn syrup, vanilla extract, and salt. Cook, stirring constantly, for 5–7 minutes, or until the mixture thickens and turns a deep amber color. Stir in the sweetened condensed milk and cook for another 2–3 minutes, or until the mixture is thick and creamy. Remove from heat and let cool slightly.

Assemble the stuffed dates: Cut a small slit in each pitted date and stuff with a small spoonful of caramel. Cut a small square of shortbread and place on top of the caramel. Repeat with remaining dates.

Make the **chocolate** topping: In a small saucepan, heat the heavy cream over medium heat until it begins to simmer. Remove from heat and stir in the vanilla extract and chocolate chips. Stir until the chocolate is completely melted and smooth.

Dip each stuffed date into the chocolate mixture and place onto a parchment-lined baking sheet.

Sprinkle with sea salt and let cool until the chocolate hardens. You can place in the fridge to speed the process.

Serve immediately or store in an airtight container in the refrigerator for up to 5 days. Enjoy!

SCAN FOR RECIPE VIDEO

Sujuk Wellington Date

You know what the best kind of food is? The ones that taste good, look cute and are portable. This one was a big hit at the dinner table!

7 to 10 Medjool Dates

Sujuk (Turkish beef sausage or you can use summer sausage. Sujuk is just much oilier when cooked so has a nice taste)

2 squares of phyllo dough (puff pastry). I used Indo-European brand.

Half a block of Cheese. I used smoked cheddar.

1 egg

Any herbs; I used parsley. Dill would be great too!

Pit the dates and preheat the oven to 375 F (190 C).

Slice the sujuk to a size that'll fit in the date. Slice the cheese to match the medjool size. I wouldn't add too much as it'll melt outside the pastry wrap!

Chop the herbs.

Whisk the egg and set aside.

Take the phyllo squares and roll it to half the thickness. This is crucial as you don't want too much pastry to wrap the date as it expands.

Fill the date with sujuk, herbs & cheese.

Wrap the date with the dough. Use the egg wash to help the edges stick and then pinch the ends. Brush the dough wrapped dates with the egg wash.

Slice the top of the dough; I did 3 small ones.

Pop into the preheated oven for about 15–20 minutes or until golden brown. Let them cool and serve!

SCAN FOR RECIPE VIDEO

White Chocolate, Rose & Pistachio Paste Date

The amount of people who have made this recipe brings me a ton of joy. Someone even made 100 of them!

10 medjool dates, pitted

1 cup rose water

1/2 cup raw and unsalted pistachios (or ready made pistachio paste)

Pinch of salt

1/4 cup water

4 ounces white chocolate

Edible rose petals, to garnish

Soak the dates in rose water for 30 minutes. Reserve date rose water to use for another recipe.

To make the pistachio paste, boil water in a saucepan and put the pistachios in there for 2 minutes, then drain and peel the skins off.

In a food processor, combine the pistachios, 1 tsp rose water, salt, and water, and blend until a paste forms.

Dry the dates with a paper towel to remove excess moisture so the chocolate can stick.

Fill each date with the pistachio paste. Melt the white chocolate in a microwave-safe bowl, stirring every 15 seconds until fully melted.

Dip each date in the white chocolate, making sure it is fully coated. Place on a baking sheet lined with parchment paper. Sprinkle rose petals on top of each date.

Chill in the fridge for 30 minutes or until the chocolate is set. Enjoy!

SCAN FOR RECIPE VIDEO

about the author

Ayesha Erkin is a trained architect that found herself spending more late nights in the kitchen than in the studio. Her favorite type of recipe development is obsessing over one thing and making it in a 100 different ways. Prior to doing that with dates, she tested the limits of her lactose intolerance by making ice-cream weekly for half a year. She is still, unfortunately, lactose intolerant and her parents "accidentally" misplaced her ice-cream maker.

Ayesha is an immigrant of mixed Turkic and Arab heritage. She was born and raised in Pakistan, alongside living between Saudi Arabia, Germany and moved to America when she was 14. Ayesha is based between Texas and London, but you'll often find her traveling elsewhere.

Say hi at hello@ayeshaerkin.com

"Date Of The Day" has been featured in The independent, Dishoom Loves, Bon Appetit, Godt.no, Mob + more!

ACKNOWLEDGEMENTS:

A huge thank you to every single one of you that has supported me and my work. From interacting online to trying these creations in person, I wouldn't have written this book had it not been for the demand.

And now for the wonderful women who volunteered to help make this book look good:

Mackenzie Smith Kelley who photographed the stellar cover shot, alongside some more incredible snaps.
Maite Aizpurua for her on point food styling skills.
Audrey Davis for providing super cool props.
Suhaila Baheyeldin from Kohl Studio for creating the beautiful illustrations for the book and the cover art.

+ my friends and family who provided me with invaluable feedback whenever I needed it. Y'all know who you are <3

Printed in Great Britain
by Amazon

ac541e10-670a-4b21-8948-ebd31c777236R01